Bella

Bella

by
Ann Hill

The Shetland Times Ltd.
Lerwick
1993

First published by The Shetland Times Ltd., 1993

ISBN 0 900662 90 5

British Library Cataloguing-in-Publication Data

A catalogue record for this book is available from the British Library.

Printed and published by
The Shetland Times Ltd.,
Prince Alfred Street, Lerwick,
Shetland, ZE1 0EP.

1
Bella's Family

Isabella Ann Hunter was born on 11th December, 1910, a daughter for William and Andrina Hunter and a sister for Hercules (9), John William (7) and Robert (3). Three years later her fourth brother, Francis Magnus, was born and the family complete.

The Hunter Family in 1913

Back row, (left to right): William, Hercules, John William and Andrina. Front row: Isabella Ann, Robert and Francis Magnus.   *Photo: R. H. Ramsay, Lerwick*

Bella's mother was Andrina Johnson from Quam, West Sandwick, Yell, the daughter of John Johnson, fisherman, and Robina Manson.

Her father was William Hunter, son of the renowned fisherman — Hercules (Hacki) Hunter.

Bella's Family Tree

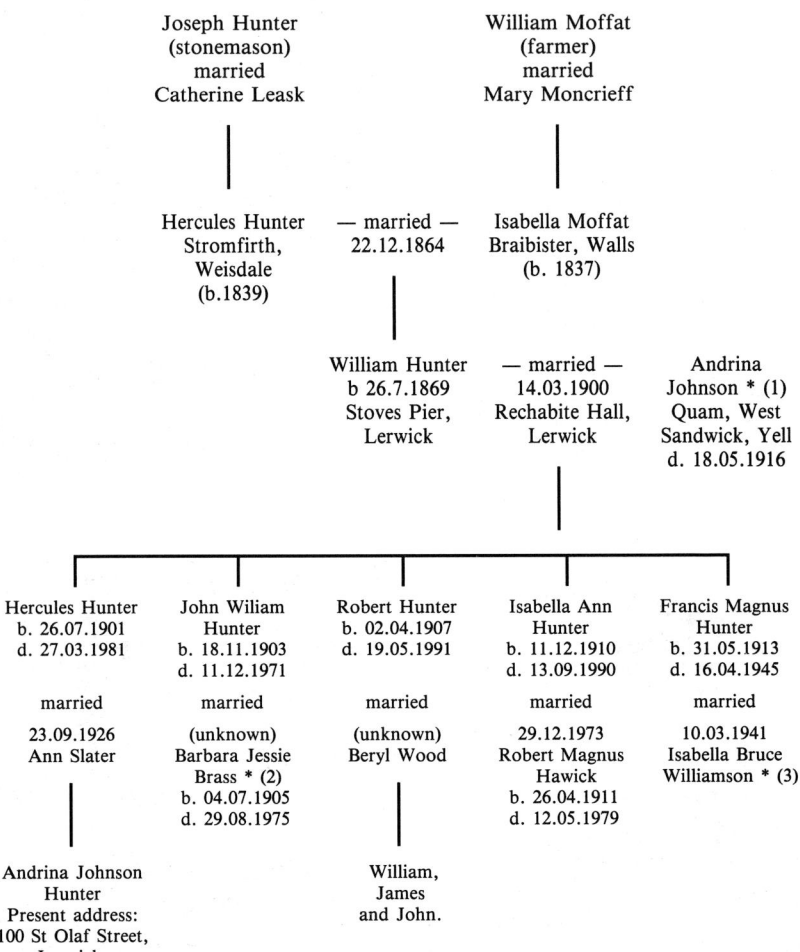

Joseph Hunter
(stonemason)
married
Catherine Leask

William Moffat
(farmer)
married
Mary Moncrieff

Hercules Hunter
Stromfirth,
Weisdale
(b.1839)

— married —
22.12.1864

Isabella Moffat
Braibister, Walls
(b. 1837)

William Hunter
b 26.7.1869
Stoves Pier,
Lerwick

— married —
14.03.1900
Rechabite Hall,
Lerwick

Andrina
Johnson * (1)
Quam, West
Sandwick, Yell
d. 18.05.1916

Hercules Hunter b. 26.07.1901 d. 27.03.1981	John Wiliam Hunter b. 18.11.1903 d. 11.12.1971	Robert Hunter b. 02.04.1907 d. 19.05.1991	Isabella Ann Hunter b. 11.12.1910 d. 13.09.1990	Francis Magnus Hunter b. 31.05.1913 d. 16.04.1945
married	married	married	married	married
23.09.1926 Ann Slater	(unknown) Barbara Jessie Brass * (2) b. 04.07.1905 d. 29.08.1975	(unknown) Beryl Wood	29.12.1973 Robert Magnus Hawick b. 26.04.1911 d. 12.05.1979	10.03.1941 Isabella Bruce Williamson * (3)

Andrina Johnson
Hunter
Present address:
100 St Olaf Street,
Lerwick.

William,
James
and John.

* (1) Andrina Johnson — daughter of John Johnson (fisherman) and Robina Manson, West Sandwick, Yell.

* (2) Barbara Jessie Brass — daughter of Peter Brass (Orkney Burgh Chamberlain) and Sarah Mary Donaldson.

* (3) Isabella Bruce Williamson — daughter of William Williamson (sawyer) and Isabella Gair.

Hercules Hunter
b. 26th July, 1901 — d. 27th March, 1981
Photo: A. & A. J. Abernethy

Robert Hunter
b. 2nd April, 1907 — d. 19th May, 1991,
Australia

Francis Magnus Hunter
b. 31st May, 1913
d. 16th April, 1945

John William Hunter
b. 18th November, 1903
d. 11th December, 1971.

2
Hercules (Hacki) Hunter

Hercules (Hacki) Hunter was born at Stromfirth, Weisdale, in 1839. When quite a young lad he prosecuted the home fishings, but soon decided to go farther afield, and in 1856 made his first voyage to the Davis Straits whale fishing in the barque *Gipsy of Peterhead*. At the outset of his career as whaler he was somewhat unfortunate, though his misfortunes resulted in a number of thrilling adventures and very narrow escapes. While crossing Melville Bay en route for the west fishing grounds in 1857, the *Gipsy* was shipwrecked. The crew were saved, however, and were taken on board the *Undaunted*, also of Peterhead, but she too was wrecked before getting across the bay. Both whalers it may be mentioned, belonged to one owner. About this time a good many iron ships were built for the seal and whale fishing and in 1858 Hunter signed on in one of these. The season proved a very successful one and Hunter rejoined her the following year, but was again destined to be in still another shipwreck, for the whaler was lost while prosecuting the seal fishing.

Hacki Hunter (centre), skipper of the "Cygnet", LK 1091, and two of his crew tarring the bushrope in 1906. *Photo: James Manson*
Photograph courtesy of Shetland Museum

Returning home Hunter found his father critically ill and he died shortly afterwards. His mother was left with 10 children, and Hunter made up his mind to do all in his power to assist them.

A new vessel, the *Lady Franklin*, built by Lady Franklin for the purpose of searching for her husband, Sir John Franklin, the explorer, arrived at Lerwick, in charge of Captain Penny on her way to the north. She was accompanied by the brig *Sofia*. Men were engaged to go on these vessels to the Cumberland Straits, and half of them were bound to remain in the Straits during the winter in order to prosecute the whale fishing with the natives in the spring. Hunter was one of the Shetland men who remained in the north and when the spring came he found ample outlet for his skill and ability, and it may truly be said of him that he was a hunter by nature as well as by name.

Captain Penny recognised him as a very capable and energetic man. Hacki continued to prosecute the seal and whale fishing for nearly 10 years onboard Captain Bruce's ship the *Camperdown*. His rating was boat steerer and harpooner, and his skill was second to none.

In the early 1870s Hunter accepted a berth as harpooner on the *S.S. Arctic* (Captain Adams), and he had a number of fortunate and remunerative trips. That his services and ability were appreciated by Captain Adams is borne out by the following extract from a report of a lecture in *The Shetland News* on 'The Polar Regions', delivered in the Town Hall, Lerwick, in March, 1887, by Captain Adams, in the course of which the lecturer said: "He looked up to some of these men (Shetlanders) he had sailed with as he had never looked up to any minister — (laughter) — and one of them particularly he must name, Hercules Hunter (applause) — a splendid fellow, and one with whom he would be only too glad to be shipmates again. With such men at his back he would not be afraid to face the largest vessel in a small cutter".

Hunter remained with Adams till 1876 when he was made second mate of the new whaler *Aurora*, under Captain Bannerman. This ship first fished at Newfoundland and thereafter at the Davis Straits. This was Hunter's last voyage but one (the exception being some years later) and on returning home he decided that he had passed enough summers in the Arctic regions, and accordingly he purchased a share in the fishing boat *Quick Step*, of which he was made skipper. He was successful in both the line and herring fishings and in subsequent years he skippered the *Beltana, Isabella* and *Neptune*. Hunter's boat was always amongst those with the highest earnings. Hunter gave up an active and eventful seafaring life only when he was 70 years of age, his remarkable vigour, strength and energy having remained practically unimpaired up to that advanced age. Idleness never appealed to him and in the evening of his life he continued actively to do odd work, such as repairs, etc., connected with fishing craft.

In the year 1862 he met with an unfortunate accident while engaged in the process of flensing a whale in the Arctic. The tackle broke and knocked him off balance. To save himself his right hand came heavily in contact with a flensing knife inflicting a serious wound. It was thought that Hunter would lose his hand, but Daniel Garster, with the aid of the medicine chest, did all he could to clean and bind up the injured hand, although Hunter suffered a great deal from the wound all the way home. He never recovered the full use of his hand and in subsequent years was compelled to fire the harpoon gun with his left hand.

Hacki Hunter was among the first Shetlanders to join the Royal Naval Reserves and he became a fully trained man.

3
Hunter and Sinclair
67 Commercial Street, Lerwick

On leaving school Bella's father, William Hunter, entered the grocery trade and was associated with it practically all his life.

He began with Hay and Co. when they had the grocery business in Commercial Street, Lerwick. Thereafter he was with Mr Fred Adie, grocer. He then went to Edinburgh where he served in several large shops before becoming manager of a business in Rose Street.

After several years in Edinburgh, William Hunter returned to Lerwick at the time when the herring fishing was booming, and for a few years acted as clerk to Mr W. J. McKay, auctioneer, who was fishsalesman for Mr W. A. A. Tulloch (Tulloch and Co.) in the years when the fish mart was at Freefield Docks, and for one season he sold herrings for Mr Tulloch. Thereafter he entered the service of Messrs John Tait and Co. who had acquired the business, referred to above, from Hay and Co. About 1902 when Messrs Tait and Co. acquired the large shop at 67 Commercial Street, Mr Hunter was appointed manager, and some six years later it was taken over by him and Mr Sinclair under the firm name of Hunter and Sinclair. Subsequently, it was conducted personally by Mr Hunter until his retiral in July, 1931, since when it was managed by his two sons, Hercules and John W. Hunter (Hacki and Jack).

William Hunter was keenly interested in the herring fishing and its development, and his earlier association with local and stranger fishermen led to an extensive business supplying the herring boats and fishergirls. He also established butcher and hardware, etc., departments, in order to supply the demands of his customers.

It may be of interest to state that William Hunter was the first grocer in the town to introduce and wear white jackets, which are now in common use in local shops.

Hunter & Sinclair, Central Supply Stores, (now the Douglas Arms public house).
Photo: Courtesy of Shetland Museum

The inside of Hunter & Sinclair, 67 Commercial Road, Lerwick.

4
The Early Years

Bella grew up in Lerwick starting school at the Lerwick Central Public School on 20th June, 1916 in class IIb.

School holidays were often spent with auntie Beena Johnson in West Sandwick, Yell.

Left: 1933, Bella Hunter, Daisy Johnson (Bella's first cousin — mother's side). Front: Andrina Johnson Hunter (Ina).

Right: Frank Hunter and Bella Hunter.

Bella left school at the age of 15 years having completed the commercial course.

Her first job was as clerkess with Walter Brown, wholesale grocer at the foot of Burgh Road, Lerwick.

She continued to work for the firm rising to become manageress until her retirement in 1973.

5
The Church

The church played an important part in Bella's life and this provided her with the start of many years of helping children through music.

The nativity play *The Three Roses* was produced by Bella alongside Joey Robertson in St Clements Hall in 1937.

This was followed by a very young Barbara Wright playing *The Matchgirl* in 1945 and *The Rag Girl* with Pryde Robertson and Anne R. Gray.

Following the war years Bella's brother John William (Jack) married Barbara Jessie Brass from Orkney. Barrie, as she was known, was the daughter of Peter Brass, Orkney Burgh Chamberlain, and Sarah Mary Donaldson.

Jack and Barrie Hunter in the garden at 29 Burgh Road, Lerwick.

Jack and Barrie took up residence with the family in 29 Burgh Road, Lerwick. Barrie was an accomplished pianist and it seemed the most natural thing to become involved in Bella's music-making projects.

Bella, along with Barrie Hunter and Joey Robertson, continued to produce for the church and in 1945 productions included the Christmas nativity play and *The Message of the Flowers*.

Nativity — "Three Roses", St Clements Hall, 1937. Back row (left to right): Ina Hunter, Betty Knight, Annie Simpson, Zeta Gray, Ivy Johnson, Sheila Cluness, Anna Birnie, Harriet Birnie, Jemima Sutherland, Bunty Blance, Netty Manson, Margaret Gray, Sheila Manson and Brenda Gray. Middle row: Betty Gray, Annie Ganson, ? Reid, Mary Moar, Ina Sandison, Carrie Gray and Georgie Leask. Front row: Betty Sutherland, Chrissie Johnson, Wilda Pole, Freda Nicolson, Betty Clark and Beatrice Clark.

14

Christmas Nativity Play, 1945. Back Row (left to right): Gracie Williamson, Lorraine Johnson, Peggy Stephen, Chrissie Johnson, Barrie Hunter, Mona Gray, Ann Gray, Maureen Cluness Pearl Jamieson, Jean Conochie, Inga Smith, Josephine Blance, Margaret Shearer, Jemima White, Bunty Malcolmson, Joyce Sim, Ishbel Sinclair, Jackie Sinclair, Carole Sinclair, Bella Hunter and Sheila Williamson. Front row: Harry Jamieson, Terry Jamieson, Jim Peterson, Dinky Spence, Alastair Fraser, Betty Sutherland, Alex Pole, Pryde Johnson.

15

The junior choir of St Columba's Church presented the cantata *The Message of the Flowers*.

The service was opened by the Church Minister, the Rev. W. Courtland B. Smith, M.B.E., who spoke of the children's enthusiasm in preparing for this event. The soloist, Master Alex Mowat, was one of the outstanding members of the choir and his clear singing was greatly enjoyed along with the other children taking part.

Tribute to the first service of its kind to be held in the Church was paid by the Sunday School Superintendent, Mr L. Cogle, who also thanked Misses Jamieson, Smith and Tulloch who had helped to decorate the church with flowers.

At the close of the service the flowers were distributed to the various institutions in Lerwick.

Among those taking part were: Bunty Malcolmson, Peggy Stephen, Mona Gray, Mona Nicolson, Jemima White, Pearl Jamieson, Pryde Robertson, Joyce Sim, Lillian Smith, Josephine Blance, Ann Gray, Margaret Shearer, Maureen Cluness, Thelma Martin, Jean Conochie, Inga Smith, Ishbel Sinclair, Jackie Sinclair, Beryl Smith, Margaret Groat, Andrew White, Alastair Fraser, Jim Spence, Benny Manson, Alex Pole, Jim Peterson, Ray Leask, Elaine Leask, Irene Bain, Barbara Wright, Robert Tulloch, George Wright, Ian McAlpine, Carol Sinclair, Robert Ollason, Sheila Williamson, Grace Williamson, George Wilson and Lorraine Johnson.

"Message of the Flowers", St Columba's Church, Lerwick, 1946.

Joey Robertson, Barrie Hunter and Bella Hunter.   Photo: Frank Scott

Pryde Robertson, Lillian Smith, Pearl Jamieson and Josephine Blance.

Lorraine Johnson, George Wilson, Grace Williamson, Sheila Williamson,
Robert Ollason and Carole Sinclair.

17

Ishbel Sinclair.

Jackie Sinclair.

Pryde Robertson, Maureen Cluness, Margaret Shearer and Anne Gray.

18

Mona Gray, Peggy Stephen, Bunty Malcolmson, Mona Nicolson and Jemima White.

Jackie Sinclair, Ishbel Sinclair and Margaret Groat.

Ian McAlpine, Robert Tulloch, George Wright, Barbara Wright, Irene Bain and Elaine Leask.

Thelma Martin, Jean Conochie and Inga Smith.

Back row: Benny Manson, Jim Spence, Alastair Fraser. Front row: Jim Peterson, Alex Pole, Ray Leask and Alex Mouat.

6
The Girl Guides

Shortly after the end of World War II Barrie Hunter, with the aid of Bella, restarted the Girl Guide Movement in Lerwick. They took great pride in teaching the girls dancing and singing.

A few years later it was felt by the Guide Movement that perhaps too much singing and dancing was being taught and not enough "guiding" and it was at this point that Bella and Barrie left the Girl Guides to form the Lerwick Girls' Choir. Many of the girls involved in Girl Guides also joined the choir.

It is interesting to note that guides of today have "entertaining" as one of their badges.

Bella and Barrie Hunter were simply ahead of their time.

Guide Anniversary, 1949/50. Relay race starting in Shetland, the most northerly post, the scroll was to be carried to London. From left: Amy Smith, Laura Smith, Janet Pottinger, Bunty Arthur (Sea Ranger), Mrs Cooper (County Commissioner), Maisie Shearer (Sea Ranger Captain), and Barrie Hunter.

The Lerwick Girls' Choir met every Friday evening in Islesburgh House. In the early 1950s Islesburgh House was still part of the school. Music score sheets were not easily come by and proved to be quite expensive.

Not to be put off, Bella would write all the words of the songs on to the school blackboard and each girl would sit at a desk and copy them down in their notebooks.

1st Guide and Brownie concert in Garrison Theatre, 1947.

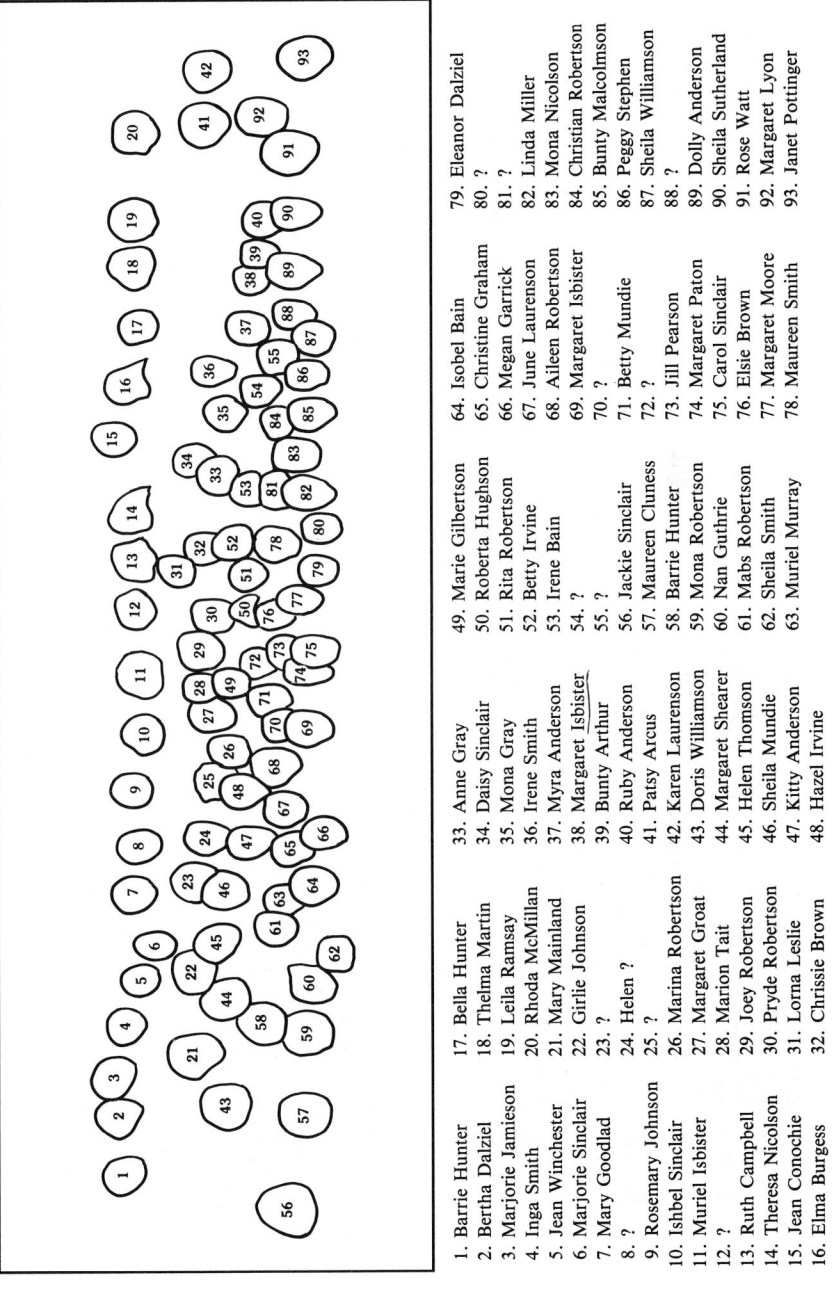

1. Barrie Hunter
2. Bertha Dalziel
3. Marjorie Jamieson
4. Inga Smith
5. Jean Winchester
6. Marjorie Sinclair
7. Mary Goodlad
8. ?
9. Rosemary Johnson
10. Ishbel Sinclair
11. Muriel Isbister
12. ?
13. Ruth Campbell
14. Theresa Nicolson
15. Jean Conochie
16. Elma Burgess

17. Bella Hunter
18. Thelma Martin
19. Leila Ramsay
20. Rhoda McMillan
21. Mary Mainland
22. Girlie Johnson
23. ?
24. Helen ?
25. ?
26. Marina Robertson
27. Margaret Groat
28. Marion Tait
29. Joey Robertson
30. Pryde Robertson
31. Lorna Leslie
32. Chrissie Brown

33. Anne Gray
34. Daisy Sinclair
35. Mona Gray
36. Irene Smith
37. Myra Anderson
38. Margaret Isbister
39. Bunty Arthur
40. Ruby Anderson
41. Patsy Arcus
42. Karen Laurenson
43. Doris Williamson
44. Margaret Shearer
45. Helen Thomson
46. Sheila Mundie
47. Kitty Anderson
48. Hazel Irvine

49. Marie Gilbertson
50. Roberta Hughson
51. Rita Robertson
52. Betty Irvine
53. Irene Bain
54. ?
55. ?
56. Jackie Sinclair
57. Maureen Cluness
58. Barrie Hunter
59. Mona Robertson
60. Nan Guthrie
61. Mabs Robertson
62. Sheila Smith
63. Muriel Murray

64. Isobel Bain
65. Christine Graham
66. Megan Garrick
67. June Laurenson
68. Aileen Robertson
69. Margaret Isbister
70. ?
71. Betty Mundie
72. ?
73. Jill Pearson
74. Margaret Paton
75. Carol Sinclair
76. Elsie Brown
77. Margaret Moore
78. Maureen Smith

79. Eleanor Dalziel
80. ?
81. ?
82. Linda Miller
83. Mona Nicolson
84. Christian Robertson
85. Bunty Malcolmson
86. Peggy Stephen
87. Sheila Williamson
88. ?
89. Dolly Anderson
90. Sheila Sutherland
91. Rose Watt
92. Margaret Lyon
93. Janet Pottinger

23

T. M. Y. Manson, Boys' Brigade Bandmaster, with Gibby Pottinger on drums, 1944.

Barrie Hunter, Rhoda McMillan and Ruby Anderson, with Guides and 2nd pack Brownies, 1944.

1st Lerwick Guides, 1947, Central School, back row (left to right): Muriel Isbister, Morag McMillan, Rosemary Johnson, Theresa Nicolson, Leila Nicolson, Leila Ramsay, Berth Dalziel, Mary Goodlad, Elma Burgess, Effie Slater and Ruth Campbell. Fourth row: Ishbel Sinclair, Mary Mainland, Ena Pearson, Myra Anderson, Jacky Sinclair, Joey Robertson, Jacqueline Irvine, Karen Laurenson and Marion Tait. Third Row: Patsy Arcus, Ann Gray, Hazel Irvine, Margaret Groat, Barbara Fraser, Janet Pottinger, Rosemary Watt, Irene Spence, Lorna Leslie, ? Smith, Mona Robertson, Chrissie Brown and Margaret Shearer. Second row: Marjory Jamieson, Bunty Arthur, Jean Winchester, Agnes Burgess, Rhoda McMillan, Barrie Hunter, Bella Hunter, Sylvia Spence, Inga Smith and Ruby Anderson. Front row: Margaret Lyon, Eva Goudie, Kitty Anderson, Wendy Hughson, Barbara Thomson, Dolly Anderson, Helen Thomason, Margaret Isbister and Doris Williamson.   Photo: R. H. Ramsay

On a Saturday afternoon it was back to Islesburgh House again for Scottish country dance lessons.

Bella continued her association with the church and in 1958 the Sunday School children, under the guidance of their Sunday School teacher, performed the Nativity Play which was "dreamed" by three children who played parts in the opening and closing scenes.

The cast included:

Three children	—	Eileen Williamson, Janet Bain and Stewart Angus.
Adult	—	Sandra Eunson
Nurse	—	Alison Rhind
Wise Men	—	James Robertson, John Johnston and James Halcrow.

Shepherds	—	Ernest Lockwood, Eric Johnson, Rognvald Mathewson and Brian Robertson.
Mary	—	Margaret Sutherland
Joseph	—	Alison Rhind
Seraph	—	Cynthia Williamson
Angels	—	Caroline Brown, Lynn McConnan, Inger Lie, George Isbister, Lorna Sinclair, Jane Spence, Elizabeth Duthie, Rae Crooks, Audrey Thomson, Sylvia Sinclair, Heather MacRae, Jennifer Williamson and Anne Spence.

They were assisted by Ann Gray, Lorraine Johnson, Sheila Johnson and Osla Robertson who also formed the off-stage choir.

Lighting was done by Mr James Halcrow and the elaborate staging was by Mr James Bolt.

7
The Lerwick Girls' Choir

"There go the Williamson lasses" said Mum, as I sat by the window watching with envy as they passed up Cairnfield Road from their house in South Lochside. Jenny, Christine, Eileen and Cynthia.

It seemed so unfair. Why was Jenny allowed to go and I wasn't? She was my friend and we normally did everything together. The reason was simple — Jenny was seven and I was still just six years old.

Every Friday night and Saturday afternoon for the next year I pined away the time until at last it had arrived — my seventh birthday — the day I had been waiting for.

Mum dressed me in my best coat and hat and holding on tightly to Cynthia Williamson's hand, we set off.

Islesburgh House seemed terribly big . . . room seven — this was it. The door opened and there it was, the thing I wanted most for my seventh birthday — Bella Hunter. I had heard all about her from Jenny Williamson.

"Could I sing" was the question she asked. Well, I managed to scrape out a verse of *Jesus Loves Me* and it must have sounded all right to Bella for I was given the treasured honour of becoming a member of the Lerwick Girls' Choir led by Bella Hunter.

Barrie Hunter, who accompanied on the piano, was affectionately known to the lasses as "Captain" (carried on from her days in the Guides).

I joined the dancing classes the next day. At last, I was one of Bella Hunter's lasses. It was 1957.

Lerwick Girls' Choir, 1958, back row (left to right): Cynthia Williamson, June Moore, Emily Anderson, Wilma Smith, Margaret Sutherland, Osla Robertson and Eleanor Barrie. Middle row: Thelma Thistlewaite, Inger Lie, Sonja Ratter, Elizabeth Gray, Eileen Williamson, Margaret West and Lynn McConnan. Front row: Olive Thistlewaite, June Young, Jennifer Williamson, Christine Manson, Jasmine Gray and Ann Laurenson.   *Photo: Dennis Coutts*

The Lerwick Girls' Choir took part in many of the music festivals held in Lerwick. There were often no other junior choirs to compete against and therefore they were expected to compete against the choirs from the SWRI and other "older" choirs. Bella's lasses received one of the highest scores ever recorded for a song called *Hickory Dickory Dock.* Other winning pieces included *A Shepherd Keeps Sheep* and *Mairi's Wedding* with marks of 86 and 89 out of a possible 100 in 1953.

Other successes included: *The Dancers* sung by Betty and Sheila Mundie (marks — 81), *Shepherd, Shepherd, Leave Your Labours* sung by Wilma Smith and Eleanor Paton (marks — 84), *Sing a Song of Spring* and *Hungarian Dance No. 5* sung by the Lerwick Girls' Choir (marks 84 and 87 respectively).

Bella's lasses were regular visitors all over the islands. The annual spring bulb show of the Scalloway SWRI was a regular event for the choir.

Many nights were spent with the old folks who stayed in Viewforth, Montfield, Leog, the old Gilbert Bain, Brevik and

The Lerwick Girls' Choir at Scalloway on Friday, 24th March, 1960.
Photo: C. J. Williamson

Scalloway Old Folks' Homes. The visit of "their lasses" was always a joyous occasion and return visits were looked forward to and many friendships made.

Seasickness was tolerated as we set off to entertain not only in the island halls such as Burra (before the bridges) but also on several visiting cruise liners, The Royal National Mission to Deep Sea Fishermen, Queen Elizabeth Institute, Lerwick, celebrated its first anniversary on 27th April, 1963, with Mr Charles Laurie, Mission Secretary, from London in attendance.

The choir sang — *These Are The Lovely Things, My Prayer, The Stars Sang in God's Garden,* and *Evensong.* The junior group sang — *Say A Little Prayer* and the senior group sang *All In The April Evening* and *Bless This House.* Wilma Smith and Elizabeth Gray sang a duet called *Think of Me.* Wilma Smith also sang a solo entitled *The Holy City.*

Also taking part was James Halcrow on pianoforte. In attendance was Provost Gray.

Bella was a keen Scottish country dancer and teacher and many of the girls from the choir also joined her dancing teams.

She would often go to St Andrews to attend dancing school and Beryl Thompson was lucky enough (and talented) to be asked to go with Bella on several occasions to polish up and learn more about Scottish country dancing.

28

Barrie Hunter (Captain) with the choir and Bella at the 1st anniversary concert of the RNMDSF, 27th April, 1963. Back row (left to right): Emily Anderson, Wilma Smith, Eleanor Barrie, June Moore and Valerie Hawick. Middle rows: Elizabeth Gray, Barbara Berrie, Jane Spence, Christine Manson, Ann Laurenson, Eileen Tait, Joyce Tait, Olive Thistlewaite, Jasmine Gray, June Robertson and Bella Hunter. Front row: Barrie Hunter, Marlene Simpson, June Young, Kathleen Leask, Harriet Robertson and Jenny Williamson.

Junior team dancing at Scalloway.   *Photo: C. J. Williamson*

Queen Mother's visit, King George V Park, Lerwick.   *Photo: E. SInclair*

One of the first dances we all learnt was *Petronella* — Kathleen Leask would lead off, turn into the middle, turn to the opposite side, turn back to your own place, four pah-de-bah, etc. etc.

Lynn McConnan, Emily Anderson, Cynthia Williamson, Beryl Thomson, Rita Quilliam, Eleanor Barrie, Eileen Williamson and Elizabeth Gray.

30

Back row (left to right): Marguerite Lynch, June Young, Olive Thistlewaite and Christine Manson. Front row: Jennifer Williamson, Jasmine Gray, Barbara Berry, Kathleen Leask and Ann Laurenson.

Back row: Julie Leith, Ann Walker, Yvonne Drever, Bella Hunter, Helen Simpson and Christine Williamson. Front row: Christine MacLeod, Angela Irvine, Marion Young, Fiona Kerr and Janice Davidson.

31

Back row: Olive Thistlewaite, Harriet Robertson, Christine Manson and Annette Balfour. Front row: Jasmine Gray, Jennifer Williamson, Margaret West and Kathleen Leask.

8
Concerts

The Lerwick Girls' Choir and the dancing teams appeared regularly at the Garrison Theatre. Variety concerts with Gordon "Hank" Smith and Allan Anderson, Tom Georgeson and Tammy Anderson.

In 1962 Islesburgh House entertained to help raise funds for the Shetland Swimming Pool Association.

The programme read: Meet the Fiddlers: Scots Reel, Strathspey and Reels and Pipe March Selection; A Musical Medley: The Lerwick Girls' Choir; *The Foula Reel* sung by "Da Boys"; Islesburgh Country Dance Team, *Isles of Skye, Waverley, Light and Airy, Mairi's Wedding* and *Letham Ladies*; Glamour and Magic from the East — El Mystico and Salome; Just a Song — Larry Peterson; Four Hits and a Miss — The Rhythm Aces; Musical Gems — The Sapphires; Tingwall's Heilan' Laddie — Ian Burns; *Somewhere a Voice is Calling* — Wilma and Osla; The Papa Stour Sword Dance — The Islesburgh House Youth Club; The Fiddlers Again — Glasgow Highlanders, Pipe Marches and Greenland Tunes. Stage Manager — Bertie Tait. Electricians — Billy Gifford and Wilbert Henry.

The Papa Stour Sword Dance performed by Islesburgh House Youth Club: John Watt, Jackie Sinclair, John Halcrow, Larry Peterson, Ronnie Sharman, John Watt and John Mouat.   *Photo: Dennis Coutts*

Pearl the Fishermaiden
by Clementine Ward

Pearl the Fishermaiden is a story about the love of a brigand chief for a simple fishermaiden. Through trials and tribulations they went to the final scene, in which it was discovered that they were actually a prince and princess, both of whom had been "missing from home" since infancy. That, of course, led to a happy ending.

The cast:

Daddy Whelk	— Anne R. Gray
Mistress Whelk	— Wilma Smith
Pearl	— Barbara Wright
Fillette	— Margaret Sutherland
King Alphonso	— Anne W. Gray
Lorenzo	— Lorraine Johnson
Petruach	— Beatrice Garriock
Limerikius	— Cynthia Williamson
Lord Chancellor	— Mabs Robertson

Sea Nymphs/Fishermaidens/Brigands/ Courtiers — Bella's Dancers.
Music — Islesburgh Melody Players.

33

Mrs Barrie Hunter, along with Miss Bella Hunter, was responsible for the arduous work of production and arrangement. They were ably assisted by Mrs McConnon, Mrs E. Gray, Miss R. Smith and Mrs Crossan, who helped to make the dresses, and by other ladies who helped to dress the children behind the scenes.

Make up and lighting were in the hands of Mr Jerry Andrews and scenery by Mr William Johnson and Mr Joseph Kay.

Before the performance Mr Eric Gray, Chairman of the Old Peoples' Welfare Committee, said that Mrs Jack Hunter and Miss Bella Hunter, who were responsible for the production of the operettas, had intimated that they intended to donate the proceeds of both performances to the Old Peoples' Welfare Committee, particularly for the use of the Good Companions' Club. The choir had entertained members of that club on several occasions and had also sped the lonely moments of those in Brevik Hospital and other hospitals in the town. In this way the girls were given an opportunity to show what they were made of, and to express any talents they had in this direction, and Mr Gray was sure that the audience would appreciate their efforts.

"Pearl the Fishermaiden": Osla Robertson, Beatrice Garriock, Cynthia Williamson, Mabs Robertson, Anne W. Gray, Jasmine Gray, Margaret Sutherland, Sheila Johnson and Elizabeth Gray.   *Photo: E. Sinclair*

"Pearl the Fishermaiden": Anne W. Gray, Jasmine Gray, Mabs Robertson, Margaret Sutherland and Beatrice Garriock.   *Photo: E. Sinclair*

Cast from "Pearl the Fishermaiden" including (far left): Barbara Wright as Pearl and Lorraine Johnson as Lorenzo.   *Photo: E. Sinclair*

35

Peach Blossom

The setting for the operetta *Peach Blossom* is the court of the Emperor of Japan, and the story revolved around the finding of a nightingale, which the Emperor had never seen.

Act one takes place in the Emperor's garden, when he ordered that the nightingale be found or dire penalties would befall the courtiers.

A wood is the setting for the second act, and the fairies entered carrying lit oriental lanterns into the gloom of the trees. Peach Blossom, a servant girl at the palace, stopped on her way home to listen to the nightingale which sang after she had played with it. Hi-Ti and Ching-Ching arrived on the scene in search of the nightingale, and Peach Blossom revealed that she knew where it was. She was immediately commanded to return with them to the Emperor.

Act three reverted to the garden, when Ching-Ching and Hi-Ti tried to tell the Emperor that they had found the bird, but they were exposed and the true finder, Peach Blossom, was brought to court.

The Emperor fell in love with her and they married, much to the delight of the fairies and flowers, but to the disgust of the ladies and gentlemen of the court.

Back row (left to right): Elizabeth Gray, Joan Anderson, Mary Craigie, Kathleen Crossan and Valerie Hawick. Front row: Sylvia Sinclair, Jasmine Gray and Christine Williamson.

The cast:

Emperor	— Lorraine Johnson
Fusi Yama	— Carole Sinclair
Ching-Ching	— Eleanor Paton
Hi-Ti	— Wilma Smith

The cast from "Peach Blossom", back row (left to right): Christian Robertson, Elaine Leask, Margaret Sutherland, Mabs Robertson, Eleanor Paton, Lorraine Johnson, Barbara Wright, Carole Sinclair, Eileen Williamson, Lynn Moar, Peggy Young, Ann Gray, Wilma Smith, Osla Robertson and Irene Bain. Front row: Lynn McConnan, Jasmine Gray, Sylvia Sinclair, Valerie Robertson, Elizabeth Gray, Margaret Craigie, Susan Wishart, Cynthia Williamson, Vaila Wishart, Joan Anderson, Kathleen Crossan, Valerie Hawick, Christine Williamson, Emily Anderson and Eleanor Barrie.

Peach Blossom — Barbara Wright
The Nightingale — Cynthia Williamson
Ladies/gentlemen of the court and fairies — Bella's Lasses.

"Peach Blossom", Wilma Smith and Eleanor Paton.

Susan Wishart, Lorraine Johnson, Barbara Wright and Vaila Wishart.

Little Gypsy Gay
A children's operetta
Written by Molly Masters, music by Evelyn Wales.

Little Gypsy Gay is the tale of a little girl who was found by the gypsies and became the darling of the tribe and whose birthday they were celebrating.

The chief of the tribe presented her with a necklace which had been found with her and which they had kept for this occasion.

A lady and gentleman appear on the scene and recognise the little girl as their long lost daughter by the necklace.

Amidst joy and sorrow, caused through her being re-united with her parents, and the fact that the tribe were to lose her, she leaves them with promises of frequent visits.

The cast:

Romany Rof	—	Lorraine Johnson
Marta	—	Barbara Wright
Thirza	—	Margaret Young
Gay	—	Margaret Sutherland
Col. James Pratt	—	Anne Gray
Mrs Angela Pratt	—	Carole Sinclair

Chorus of Gypsies:

Jorga	—	Lynn Moar
Mick	—	Eleanor Paton
Marko	—	Wilma Smith
Anyeta	—	Cynthia Williamson
Tarna	—	Eileen Williamson
Zingra	—	Osla Robertson
Marisescu	—	Christian Robertson

Mr Jerry Andrews — lighting and sound effects; Mr J. S. Hunter — painting and scenery; Mr Ronald Conochie — music; Miss Rose Smith — dresses; Mrs Crossan, Mrs McConnan, Mrs H. Hunter, Mrs L. Sinclair, Miss Anne Gray and Miss Sheena Manson — helping to dress and make up the performers.

Messrs. W. K. Conochie were responsible for the selling of tickets and the Boys' Brigade sold programmes and acted as ushers.

Princess Chrysanthemum

Princess Chrysanthemum is the story of a Princess wooed by two princes, one good and the other bad. The latter lures her to the Cave of Inky Night in an endeavour to win her, but her Good Genius rescues her, and in the end true love conquers.

The principals were supported by courtiers, fairies and sprites. The sprites were very young members, in red pixie hats and green dresses, who entered into the spirit of their "naughtiness" wholeheartedly.

There were, too, the even younger Butterflies, at least one of whom proved to be a "howling" success in mime. *The Shetland Times* reports — "during the singing they opened their mouths but forgot to close them as though singing the words! An unqualified success".

Exclamations of delight were heard with the entry of white clad, dainty fairies, played by slightly older girls.

The courtiers were attired in a variety of coloured dresses, all beautiful.

The cast:

Princess Chrysanthemum	—	Wilma Smith
Tu Lip	—	Lynn McConnan
Du Du	—	June Moore
Yum Yum	—	Elizabeth Gray
To To	—	Irene Allan
Moonbeam (Good Genius)	—	Eileen Williamson
Emperor What-For-Whi	—	Margaret Sutherland
Prince So-Tru	—	Beatrice Garriock

Prince So-Sli	— Emily Anderson
Top Not	— Osla Robertson
Saucer Eyes	— Eleanor Barrie
Fairies (senior and junior)	— Bella's Lasses
Sprites	— Bella's Lasses

Mrs Barrie Hunter — accompanist; Mr Drew Robertson and Mr Ronnie Sutherland — double bass; Rognvald Mathewson and Ernie Lockwood — sound effects; Jerry Andrews — make up; Gilbert Blance and assistants — lighting; Tony Kitson painted and shifted the very effective scenery, which included a backdrop of Fujiyama, Japan's highest mountain.

"Princess Chrysanthemum": Wilma Smith and Beatrice Garriock.

40

Photo: Dennis Coutts

Cast of "Princess Chrysanthemum".

Margaret Sutherland, Margaret West, Inger Lie, Joan Anderson and Joyce Manson.
Photo: Dennis Coutts

Eileen Williamson and Wilma Smith.   *Photo: Dennis Coutts*

42

Sprites: Margo Rintoul, Ann-Britt Smaaskjaer, Kathleen Leask, Olive Thistlewaite,
June Young, Barbara Berry, Christine Manson, Ann Laurenson, Sheila Fraser,
Jasmine Gray, Fiona Simpson and Jennifer Williamson.   *Photo: Dennis Coutts*

Fairies: Barbara Andrews, Thelma Manson, Marguerite Lynch and Elizabeth Johnson.
Front: Iris Young and Elsé Smaasjkaer.   *Photo: Dennis Coutts*

43

Back row (left to right): Patricia Sutherland, Kathleen Crossan, Eileen Williamson. Middle row: Joyce Ward, Christine Williamson, June Robertson. Front row: Valerie Hawick, Thelma Thistlethwaite, Margaret Johnson.   *Photo: Dennis Coutts*

Cinderella

written by Frank Booth

A joint production between Islesburgh Drama Group and
Lerwick Girls' Choir

The traditional fairy tale of Cinderella, the story of a young girl
whose mother dies and whose father marries again. Her two step-
sisters prove to be unfriendly.

Everyone is invited to attend the Royal Ball but Cinderella is not
allowed to go. However, with the help of her Fairy Godmother who
provides her with dress and transport, she attends the ball and falls
in love with the handsome Prince.

On leaving the ball at midnight she drops one of her glass slippers.

The Prince searches the land for the owner and finally finds that
the slipper fits Cinderella.

They marry and live happily ever after.

Cast:

Cinderella	— Wilma Smith
Prince Charming	— Margaret Sutherland
Ugly Sisters:	
Clarinda	— Allan Anderson
Miranda	— Stewart Smith
Baroness	— Anne Gray
Signor Romero	— Harry Reid
Fairy Godmother	— Emily Anderson
Fairy Queen	— Lynn McConnon
Head Cook	— Kenneth Groat

Fairies — Ann Laurenson, June Robertson, Barbara Berry, Sheila
Fraser, Olive Thistlethwaite, Jasmine Gray, Jennifer
Williamson, June Young, Valerie Hawick, Kathleen Leask,
Christine Manson

Elves — Harriet Robertson, Fiona Simpson, Anne Bain, Vera Gray,
Marion Irvine, Marlene Simpson, Ann-Britt Smaaskjaer,
Elizabeth Johnson

Assistant Cooks — Eleanor Barrie, Frances Gilbertson, Margaret
West, Margaret Gray, Sheila Henderson, Elizabeth Stevenson,
Irene Allen, June Moore, Thelma Tulloch and Jessie Smith

The show was produced by Bella Hunter and Harold Leask.

The accompanist was Mrs Jack Hunter.

Behind the scenes were: Graham Robertson, Jeff Bowers, Josie Kay,
Billy Gifford, Gilbert Blance, Billy Kay, Mrs L. F. Henry, Mrs Irvine,
Ann Gilbertson and Eileen Robertson.

Back row (left to right): Elizabeth Stevenson, Margaret Gray, Ann Gray, Sheila Henderson, Kenneth Groat, Margaret West, Eleanor Barrie, Elizabeth Gray, June Moore. Second row: Irene Allan, Harry Reid, Francis Gilbertson, Anne Gray, June Young, Lyn McConnon, Ann Laurenson, Valerie Hawick, Emily Anderson, Barbara Berry, Stuart Smith and Allan Anderson. Third row: Kathleen Leask, Sheila Fraser, Olive Thistlethwaite, Christine Manson, Jasmine Gray, June Robertson, Jennifer Williamson. Front row: Anne Bain, Vera Gray, Elizabeth Johnson, Marion Irvine, Margaret Tulloch, Wilma Smith, Else Smaaskjaer, Margaret Sutherland, Ann-Britt Smaaskjaer, Marlene Simpson, Harriet Robertson and Fiona Simpson.

46

Tell Wiz!

A Shetland musical by Harry Kay and Ronnie Mathewson

Tell Wiz! was a Shetland musical written by Harry Kay and Ronnie Mathewson depicting Arctic whaling days, the Baker's Waal in Baker's Kloss, the halcyon days of the herring fishing both at Freefield Docks (the original "Docks Bell" being used) and at the Esplanade "new" fishmarket (now no more), and the Market Green.

The cast:

Janie	— Miss Nan Goudie
Neenie	— Miss Minnie Wright
Kirsty	— Miss Beth Goudie
Osla	— Miss Jessie Smith
Mary Jean	— Miss Barbara Wright
Beenie	— Miss Ann Gray
Babsy: Lady Perskeet	— Mrs Mona Dalziel
Tamar	— Mrs Roby Peterkin
Merrin	— Mrs Harriet Mathewson
Norma	— Miss Leila Young
Aggie	— Miss Marie Gilbertson
Erty	— Mr Tom Georgeson
Hakki	— Mr Jack Hunter
Jessie Mary; Liza: Geedian	— Mr Stewart Smith
Donzie	— Mr Larry Peterson
Mansie	— Mr Laurie Dalziel
Charlie; McEwan	— Mr John Kerr
Rasmie	— Mr Harold Leask
Gibbie	— Mr Alex Gray
Simey	— Mr Allan Anderson
Hundle	— Mr Arthur Robertson
Peerie Gibbie	— Mr Ron Mathewson
Oli	— Mr D. J. H. Kay

Bella's lasses taking part in the *Capstan Dance*: Cynthia Williamson, Beryl Thomson, Eileen Williamson, Margaret Sutherland, Eleanor Barrie, Wilma Smith, Lynn McConnon and Emily Anderson.

Fiddler: Mr Arthur Roberson.

Girls trained by Miss Bella Hunter and Mrs J. Hunter.

Stage Manager	— Mr Harold Leask
Stage Carpenter	— Mr Joseph Kay
Lighting and effects	— Mr Graham Robertson and Jimmy McCall
Make-up	— Mr Jerry Andrews
Materials	— Mr R. Burgoyne, hairdresser

Docks Bell Scene: All properties, including oilskins, loaned by Mr Frank Garriock of Messrs Hay and Co. (Lerwick) Ltd.

Capstan Dance — Tell Wiz!: Cynthia Williamson, Emily Anderson, Margaret Sutherland, Wilma Smith, Beryl Thomson, Eileen Williamson, Lynn McConnon.

Tell Wiz! Islesburgh Drama Group with Bella's lasses in the front.

Photo: E. Sinclair

48

The Sound of Music

An Islesburgh Drama Group production
Music by Richard Rodgers
Lyrics by Oscar Hammerstein II

28/29/30 September, 1978

The Islesburgh Drama Group production of the *Sound of Music* saw Bella taking part as one of the nuns.

This was a rare appearance of Bella "on stage". She was not the type of person who liked to be "seen", being more comfortable behind the scenes.

Photo: Dennis Coutts

Cast:

Maria Rainer, a Postulant in Nonneberg Abbey —
    Catherine Willn
Sister Berthe, Mistress of Novices —   Ivy Cluness
Sister Margaretta, Mistress of Postulants —
    Elizabeth Williamson
Mother Abbess —   Daphne Moss
Sister Sophia —   Abigale Skinner
Captain Georg Von Trapp —   Donald McLeay
Franz, the butler —   Stanley Manson
Frau Schmidt, the house keeper —   Lorna Pole

Children of Von Trapp —
    Gretl —   Nora Barnes
    Marta —   Ingrid Malcolmson
    Kurt —   Melvyn Leask
    Brigitta —   Lauris Black
    Louisa —   Grace Barnes
    Friedrich —   Brian Groat
    Liesl —   Janet Moss

Rolf Gruber —   Dennis Cumming
Elsa Schraeder —   Brenda Overend
Max Detweiler —   Derick Herning
Herr Zeller —   Alan Cross
Baron Elberfeld —   John Mustard
A Postulant —   Joyce Thomson
Admiral Von Schreiber —   Kenneth Watt

Nuns —
Ann Sandison, Joyce Thomson, Bella Hunter, Julia Gibson, Ina Hunter, Abigale Skinner, Ivy Cluness, Nancy Alan, Celia Barnes, Elizabeth Williamson, Marion Ockendon, Wilma Halcrow, Dorothy Stove, Catherine Scott, Margaret Young, Fiona Macpherson, Lilian Gibson, Judith Bayles, Pat Ferris, Jean Hutchieson

— including members of Lerwick Choral Society

Produced by	— Donald McLeay
Musical Director	— Elizabeth Kerr
Assisted by	— Robin Barnes

Orchestra:

Conducted by Elizabeth Kerr

1st Violins	— Rodger Wildman Eleanor Reid
2nd Violins	— Vera Johnston Bernadette Porter
Flutes	— Barney Leith Fiona Forbes
Cello	— Pam Smith
Double Bass	— Mike Blyth
Clarinet	— Tommy Sutherland
Trumpets	— Niall Cruickshank Alan Irvine
Trombone	— Drew Robertson
Oboe	— Margaret Rushton
Pianist	— Robin Barnes
Percussion	— Douglas Johnstone

Stage Crew —	Joe Kay, Kenneth Groat, Stephen McKay
Lighting Crew —	Ian Smith, Sandy Simpson
Scenery Artist —	Morag McGill
Costumes —	Ellen Irvine
Props —	Sheila Robb, Fiona McAdie
Make Up —	Alan Cross

51

9
29 Burgh Road, Lerwick

Choir practices were often held in 29 Burgh Road, Lerwick. The lasses would gather around the piano played by "Captain" in the sitting room. It was a very comfortable room with lots of chairs and a china cabinet, full of beautiful ornaments including glasses which Bella had painted pictures of crinoline ladies onto.

Tea and cakes would be served by Leebie Robertson. Leebie had arrived as housekeeper to the Hunter family after the death of Bella's mother Andrina in 1916.

Leebie Robertson on her 80th birthday with "Chum" the family pet (Shetland Collie) who was always a great favourite with the lasses.

Leebie died on 26th February, 1961 aged 95 years.

10
Summer Carnivals

The midsummer carnival in Lerwick was always enthusiastically entered into, the lorry brightly decorated and everyone dressed up. We sang all around the route.

George Batty jumped onto the lorry beside Lynn McConnan just to have his photo taken with Bella's lasses.   *Photo: E. Sinclair*

Summer picnics were an annual event. Frying sausages at Kergord and Bressay, treasure hunts at Bigton, the choir parties when Bella made sure that the boys were "suitable" before they were invited and the old gramophone which went everywhere even if it was a bit temperamental at times.

11
Up-Helly-A'

As a young lady Bella enjoyed Up-Helly-A', dancing in the halls.

Y.M.C.A. Up-Helly-A' 1935 or 1936. Leebie Robertson (arrowed), the Hunter's Housekeeper after Andrina Hunter died in 1916.

Islesburgh boys. Back row (left to right): Roy Greenwald, Bobby Smith, Alan Thomson, Kenny Crossan, Campbell Johnson, Hughbert Brown. Front row: Larry Williamson, John Watt, Larry Peterson, John Watt, Jackie Sinclair, Ronnie Sharman.

Her involvement in later years from being a hostess in the Central School to teaching "her boys" the steps and routines for their squad acts.

The old Islesburgh House boys were one of her regular squads. She would teach the boys the steps of the dances until they were step perfect. If you were lucky enough to get an invitation to the Central School on Up-Helly-A' night you were assured of a great performance from Bella's boys. She had more than one squad but in her quiet unassuming way, you were never sure how many or even who. After all, Bella was strong on tradition, it was a secret between her and Up-Helly-A'.

Back row (left to right): ?, Alan Thomson, Jim Burgess, Hugh Jamieson, Kenny Crossan, Campbell Johnson, George Barrie, John Mowat, Danny Baxter, Hughbert Brown. Middle row: Alex Goudie, Mitnie Simpson, John Watt, Jackie Sinclair, Stanley Sinclair, John Watt, Ronnie Sharman, Bobby Smith. Front row: Larry Peterson, Graham Jeffrey, Jack Greenwald, John Halcrow.   *Photo: Dennis Coutts*

Bella's Boys

Contributed by Stanley Manson

In 1975 one of Lerwick's longest serving Up-Helly-A' squads, under the leadership of Harry Jamieson, was vainly trying to learn the steps of a minuet to accompany the very attractive suits of the Wombles, but deary me, 24 men fumbling around the hall just could make nothing of it. John Allan, as usual, had a bright idea. "We need Bella", he said.

Bella Hunter stayed next door to John and was delighted to come and help. Can you picture the scene — the likes of Tiny Jamieson, Hammy Gifford, Jim Nicolson, Tootsie Gray (in his wellies) and George Hepburn (not the smallest of men) being put through their paces by the delicate and delightful Bella?

This was to be the start of a permanent association with Bella and her "squad". During the following years Bella was always at hand to give her boys help and in 1977 the suit was Mini Scots — a big busbie covering most of the body with a face painted on the bellies and a mini kilt completed the suit — a routine was required and Bella came up trumps with position drill and a *Highland Fling.*

In 1980 an idea had been seen by someone on holiday — Bamboo Dancers — and even although Bella had never seen this, she made a dance up of intricate steps between poles on the floor. It was said that the act was as good at the last hall as at the first with the whole squad keeping perfect timing between the poles — even with a dram!

In 1982 the *Birdie Dance* made its debut and her now dancing squad were first to get the name in. With Bella's help again the act was planned and the "Tweets" and the audiences danced the night away.

Bella was at hand again when in 1984 the suit was that daft duck "Orville". What could the dance be for this? You just have to believe it — *Swan Lake* ballet. Stanley Manson even had to go to her house for lessons — eat your heart out Rudolf Nureyev. Another hit suit and act — thanks to Bella.

Furry suits and dances are now legendary with the squad and in 1986 we saw the arrival of the kids' hit programme "Care Bears". John Allan moulded a perfect head and again Bella choreographed an unfaltering *May Pole Dance* which delighted the audiences around the halls.

1990 brought Bella back with the boys again — this time to train 24 "My Little Ponies" into the *Palais Glide* and as usual after many rehearsals Bella had them moving in perfect(?) unison which they vainly tried to continue throughout the evening.

The Muppets 1978.   *Photo: Dennis Coutts*

Wombles 1975.   *Photo: Dennis Coutts*

This year was the fifteenth year of involvement with Bella and her squad and to mark the occasion she was presented with a silver pony brooch from the boys.

Members of the squad over the years were:

Harry Jamieson	John Allan	John Anderson
Jimmy Sim	Magnie Sim	Alex Sim
Stanley Manson	Richie Simpson	Tony Ryder
Frank Pearson	Wibby Couper	Gary Couper
John Tulloch	Jo Gray	Hamilton Gifford
George Hepburn	Norman Smith	Tommy Jamieson
Jimmy Davidson	David Davidson	Jim Nicolson
Kenny Nicolson	Gibby Blance	Ian Blance
Johnny Wiseman	Leonard Jamieson	John Jamieson
Eddie Reid	Jim Birnie	

12
Tingwall Ladies
Contributed by Lillian Leslie

Once a year in the Tingwall Hall the men take over the kitchen and do the cooking and serving for a dinner-dance. Not to be outdone, as a reply to the "Men's Night", the "Ladies' Night" was born.

As a variation from the normal dinner dance, the ladies choose a theme for the evening, and have worked their way through several countries. The meal, hall decoration and the ladies themselves dress up in the costume of the chosen country, and have a "spot" during the evening when they do a dance traditional to the chosen theme.

The Tingwall ladies approached Bella to see if she could help with a formation dance suitable for a Spanish evening. She immediately agreed, although they learned later that she wasn't in good health.

She was very enthusiastic as usual and soon choreographed a dance routine and put them through their paces.

The Tingwall ladies include: Kathleen Balfour, Margaret Nicolson, Thelma Leslie, Lillian Leslie, Andrea Jeromson, Liz Garrick, Jean Sandison, Jane Sharp, Pearl Johnson, Eleanor Leslie, Anita Polson, Hazel Sinclair and Laureen Slater.

Tingwall Ladies, February 1990.

13
The Church

The Church played an important part throughout Bella's life. In later years the Lerwick Girls' Choir reformed to take part in the Congregational Church programme on Sunday, 21st December, 1986. The songs they sang included some old favourites: *Mary's Boy Child, Silent Night, In Bethlehem, Ding Dong Merrily on High, Rejoice Good Christian People* and *Jingle Bells*.

On 25th May, 1987 the Rev David Monkton, Minister to the Methodist Church in Lerwick wrote to Bella: —

Dear Bella,

I would be pleased if you would pass on to the Girls' Choir our appreciation of the excellent singing we were able to enjoy listening to last night when they came to sing at our weekly "Songs of Praise".

We all felt it was a very worthwhile evening which was very considerably enhanced by the Lerwick Girls' Choir's contributions in song. We hope that one of these days it might be possible for you to come again.

With all good wishes,
Yours sincerely,
David Monkton.

Bella's commitment to her Church was total. She taught in Sunday School and was a lifelong member of St Columba's Church Choir.

She also enjoyed the regular choir outings.

150th Anniversary, Lerwick Parish Church 1979. Back row (left to right): Mona Tulloch, Ina Tulloch, Eva Leask, Lara Inkster, Pryde Johnson, Jean Hutchison, Winnie Davidson, Bella Hawick. Middle row: Margaret Young, David Fotheringham, Bill Rhind, Tom Ramsay, George Ewan, Jim Taylor, John Manson, Margaret Manson. Front row: Daisy Williamson, Ina Hunter, Ann Halcrow, James Halcrow, Maisie Shearer, Eileen Reid, Betty Anderson.

Photo: Dennis Coutts

The choir outing to Lunna in 1969. Back row (left to right): Eileen Reid, ?, George Greig, Maisie Shearer, ?, Nancy Greig. Second row: Winnie Davidson, Eva Leask, Daisy Williamson, Joey Robertson, Barrie Hunter, Mona Gray, Bella Hunter, Anne Gray, Harry Stevenson. Middle row: Betty Anderson, Margaret Manson, Anne Gray, Willie McLennan, Jeannie McLennan, Bill Rhind. Front row: Ina Hunter, Jim Taylor, Rev Andrew Lambie, Ian Furnival, Jack Hunter.

61

14
The Choral Society

Bella was a regular performer with the Lerwick Choral Society. The 150th Anniversay of Lewick Concert of Music and Drama by Lerwick Choral Society and Islesburgh Drama Group on Friday, 14th June, 1968 brought an abundance of talent to the Lerwick stage.

A variety of songs by the Choral Society, a performance of the play *Wedding Breakfast* by William Dinner and William Morum, a farcical comedy, a piano duet by Sheila Bruce and Pearl Bartai and a further performance by the Drama Group of *Crack O' Doom*, a Scots comedy by Angus Adam, proved to be an exciting evening.

Musicians for the evening included John Tyldesley on 1st violin, Harold Stove on 2nd violin, Pearl Bartai on viola, Joanna Tyldesley on flute, Pamela Smith on cello, Ferenc Bartai on bass.

The conductor was Mrs Merle and the pianist was Mrs Sheila Bruce.

In June 1969 the Choral Society excelled in its performance of Haydn's greatest oratorio *The Creation*.

The Choral Society showed courage in deciding to engage three professional vocal soloists and to augment the local orchestra by bringing in seven instrumentalists. The choir of almost seventy voices were supported by their own accompanist at the piano and by a splendidly balanced group of 21 players.

The soloists were: soprano Patricia MacMahon; tenor Roy Benson; bass James Kelman.

The Choral Society at the performance of Haydn's oratorio "The Creation" in 1969.

The Choral Society

Choir:

Sopranos:
B. Anderson
K. A. Birnie
N. Conochie
P. D. M. Cruickshank
J. Davidson
M. R. Furnival
A. W. Gray
K. Gray
W. M. Halcrow
L. J. Henry
A. J. Hunter
B. Hunter
C. Hurlock
J. Hutchison
R. Irvine
R. C. G. Irvine
N. Jamieson
H. H. Johnson
P. A. Laurenson
A. Leask
M. L. Leask
W. J. Leask
M. K. Manson
J. Morrison
D. Ramsay
D. Ratter
E. S. Reid
A. M. Rodger
C. Spence
B. Stride
E. M. Thomson
A. Williamson

Altos:
D. B. Bulter
L. Cornes
E. C. Duthie
J. C. Forbes
N. Greig
B. J. Hunter
M. Irvine
P. Johnson
E. Leask
J. Moncrieff
E. Mullay
L. Robertson
C. Rowe
M. N. Shearer
C. Stevenson
M. Tait
M. Young

Tenors:
A. Andrews
J. Blair
I. M. Furnival
J. Gillespie
A. E. Lambie
A. S. Laurenson
I. McDill
M. Peterson
C. Stevenson
A. Twatt

Basses:
L. Butler
L. J. Dalziel
B. Edwardson
G. Greig
E. Henry
C. G. Inmam
D. F. Irving
T. G. Ramsay
S. Smith

Orchestra:

1st Violins	*Flutes*
J. Tyldesley	E. Bowie
H. Stove	J. Tyldesley
M. Banks	T. M. Y. Manson
2nd Violins	*Oboe*
B. Gray	E. Hollister
V. Johnson	
F. Bigwood	*Clarinets*
	R. Howie
Viola	T. Sutherland
J. Goodlad	
	Horns
Celli	H. Johnstone
P. Smith	M. Webster
M. Ingram	
	Trumpets
Piano	D. Robertson
S. Bruce	G. Johnson
	Trombone
	W. Dalziel

15
Hamefarin

Bella's lasses performed for the first Hamefarin in 1960 when Shetland exiles from all over the world gathered in Shetland to re-establish their Shetland roots and to visit relatives.

Hamefarin — 1960. Inger Lie, Lynn McConnan.

The choir and dancers reformed in 1985 to take part in the second Hamefarin. Favourite songs such as *Isles of Gletness, Shetland Lullaby* and *Under the Old Linden Tree* were accompanied by Nancy Greig and James Halcrow.

The Lerwick Girls' Choir performing for the Hamefarin 1985 video "Bon Hoga" in King George V Park, Lerwick.

Hamefarin 1985 (left to right): Jenny Wiseman, Vera Polson, Cynthia Jamieson, Beryl Burgess, Rita Williamson, Valerie Leask, Audrey Spence, Harriet Middleton, Kathleen Grant, Christine Carter.

Hamefarin 1985, Anderson High School, Lerwick. Back row (left to right): Eileen Sinclair; Cynthia Jamieson, Jennifer Wiseman, Vera Polson, Anne Mullay, June Wylie, Iris Wylie, Lynn Arcus. Second row: Elizabeth Gray, Ingrid McDonald, Emily Knight, Osla Henderson, Valerie Leask, Jasmine Moncrieff, Jane Farmer, Carol Edwardson, Audrey Spence, Wilma Halcrow. Third row: Ruby Smith, Sheila Anderson, Ann Hill, Bella Hawick, Harriet Middleton, Kathleen Grant, Ann Amedro, Dorothy Stove. Front row: Christine Manson, Joan Cameron, Janice Paton, June Black, Marion Ockendon, Margaret Angus, Sheila Newcombe.

16
Mr and Mrs Bobby Hawick

On 29th December, 1973 Bella Hunter married Robert Magnus Hawick.

Bella and Bobby courted in their younger days and although Bobby had asked for Bella's hand in marriage many times she had always said no. She had committed her life to helping the lasses grow up and to making sure that they all had the opportunity to be involved in music and dancing.

However Bobby Hawick did not give up and Bella finally said yes.

Bobby Hawick was the son of Christopher Hawick, Master Mariner, and Agnes Blance. Bobby gave up his house — Montfield House — and they set up home in 29 Burgh Road, Lerwick — Bella's family home.

Back row (left to right): Jean Mathewson, Rev Andrew Lambie, Liz Lambie, Bella Hunter (Mrs Frank Hunter), Ann Hunter, Hacki Hunter, Agnes Slater (Bobby's sister), Jack Slater. Front row: John Mathewson, Bobby Hawick, Bella Hunter, Ina Hunter.

Bella's beloved Bobby died on 12th May, 1979.

Bella did not look on her time with Bobby as short (five and a half years), rather as a bonus she had not been expecting.

17
Aunty Bella

Bella not only helped "bring up" her lasses but also their children as well.

"Wir bairns" were always brought to Aunty Bella for approval and she loved them all as if they were her own.

Bella Hawick with Catriona Hill, April, 1984.

18
Australia

Bella's brother Robert (Bobby) emigrated to Australia in 1927. Bobby's family very quickly became part of Bella's life and in March 1988, accompanied by her niece Ina Hunter, daughter of Hacki (jnr) and Ann, set off for Australia which would soon become their second home.

Her lasses gathered to wish them bon voyage.

Bella in Gosford, New South Wales, with her brother Bobby and niece Ina Hunter, (100 St Olaf Street, Lerwick).

19
Folk Festival

Involvement in the Folk Festival was always a regular event for Bella. Home-made cakes and biscuits were always seen as ample reward by the lasses.

On 16th August 1969 the Shetland Folk Society arranged a folk concert in the assembly hall of the Anderson Educational Institute to celebrate the Shetland Quincentenary (1469 to 1969).

The Lerwick Girls' Choir sang *Da Isles o' Gletness, Baloo Balilli* and the *Shetland Lullaby*.

They were part of a concert which included the Shetland Fiddlers playing a Shetland selection, Marion Young reciting *Firelicht* by Vagaland (pen-name of T. A. Robertson), Arthur Robertson playing Shetland fiddle tunes, George Nelson speaking on the aims and achievements of the Shetland Folk Society, The Dance Team, Ann Gray singing *Da Norrowa Wheel*, a team of men from the isle dancing the Papa Stour sword dance led by George P. S. Peterson who played the traditional air on the fiddle, Wilma Young on the fiddle, Shirley Peterson, aged five, and her father Larry in a duet *Da Rabbit's Lullaby* and a quartet featuring Jim Taylor, Jack Hunter, Laurence Dalziel and David Fotheringham singing *Land of the Northmen*. Tom Georgeson played a piano solo of his own composition, the *Dotanron Hambo*, in the rhythm of the Swedish dance, the *Hambo*.

Bella continued her involvement right up to 1990 when she took her lasses to perform alongside Tom Anderson.

On stage with Tom Anderson is Jacqui Sinclair, Emma Johnston and Jeanna Johnston. Seated on the steps is Bella. Two great Shetlanders who have contributed so much to Shetland music and youth.

Photo: Douglas Grant

Back row (left to right): Kathleen Grant, Cynthia Jamieson, Rita Williamson, Jennifer Wiseman, Valerie Leask. Front row: Audrey Spence, Iris Wylie, Harriet Middleton, Vera Polson, Christine Carter.

Folk Festival 1990.

Bella was always available to help out for charity. She was a regular at church fetes, coffee mornings for organisations such as SSPCA, SWRI, Choral Society and latterly serving in the Save the Children shop on Commercial Street, Lerwick.

20
At the End of the Day

(one of Bella's favourite songs)

On 13th September, 1990, Bella Hawick died at home in 29 Burgh Road, Lerwick.

Her funeral took place in St Columba's Church, Lerwick, the church she had loved all her life. The lasses knew without a shadow of doubt that Bella would have liked her lasses to be with her.

As we sat beside her in St Columba's Church we remembered all she had taught us, "hold your heads up high and sing out clearly." We did just that but I am sure that she would have forgiven the tears.

So many of us owe our childhood upbringing, teenage years and personalities to Bella, who treated all of us like her special friend. She helped shape so many lives, taught us friendship and sharing with each other. Most of all Bella gave us the love and respect we all carry with us today.

Not just for our families but for each other.

This book is simply a tribute to Bella — our teacher and friend — from us all.

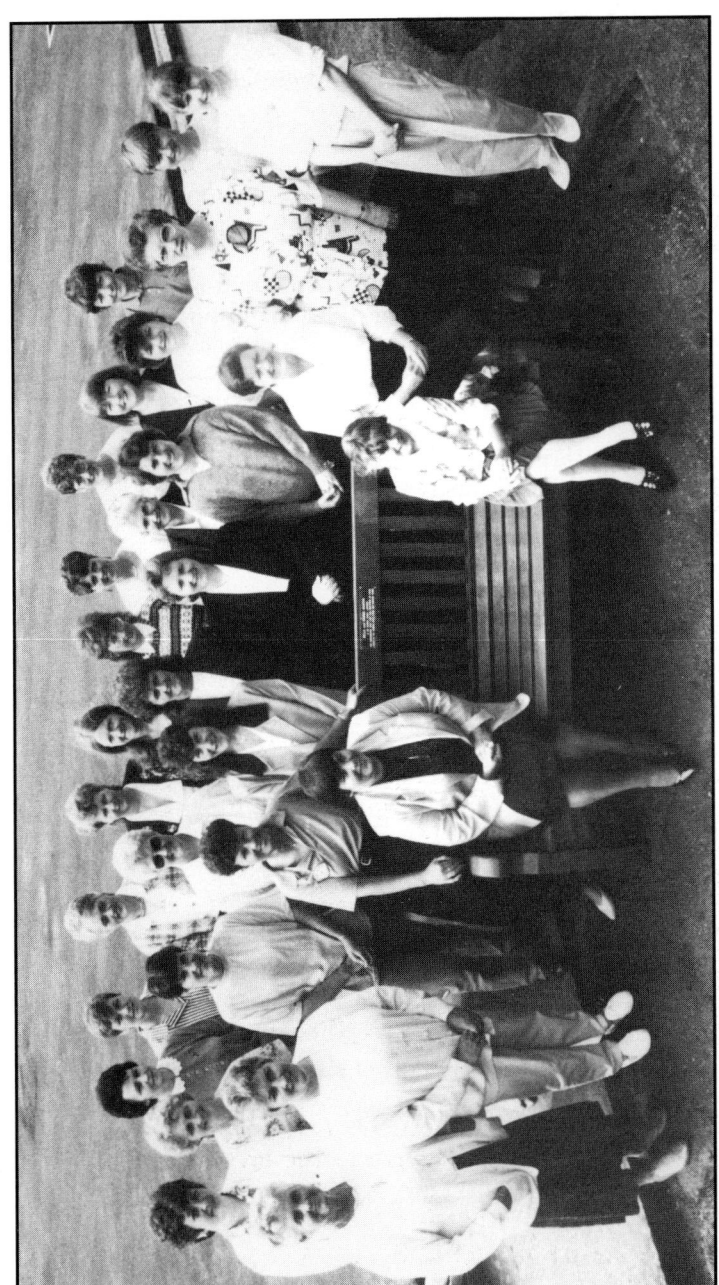

Bella's lasses gather in the King George V Park, Lerwick, to see a bench put in place in remembrance of the late Bella and Barrie Hunter. The plaque on the bench reads: "Remembered with love and gratitude by their lasses in the Lerwick girls' choir and dancing teams". The young lady in the foreground is Fiona Isabel Hill, named after Bella, whose mother, Ann, compiled this book from photographs and memories of all the girls.

Photo: Malcolm Younger

Acknowledgments

There are so many people who have helped with this book it would be impossible to name them all.

To everyone who has contributed a story, a memory or a shared moment I would simply say thank you for sharing them with me.

To everyone who has helped name faces in the photographs, I hope I have got it right but would apologise for some who may be wrong or simply missed out.

I trust everything is as near as memories will allow.

To the following I offer thanks for allowing publication of their photographic material:—

A. & A. J. Abernethy
Dennis Coutts
Douglas Grant
David Hill
R. H. Ramsay
Shetland Museum
E. Sinclair
C. J. Williamson
Ruby Williamson
Malcolm Younger

Thanks also to the Shetland Library and *The Shetland Times* for information from cuttings, etc. and for permission to use them.